Jacques OFFENBACH
OVERTURE
for
La belle Hélène

Arranged by
EDMUND HAENSCH
Edited by
Clark McAlister

Study Score
Partitur

SERENISSIMA MUSIC, INC.

ORCHESTRA

Piccolo

Flute

2 Oboes

2 Clarinets in A

2 Bassoons

4 Horns in F

2 Trumpets in C

3 Trombones

Timpani

Percussion
(Triangle, Tambourine, Snare Drum, Cymbals, Bass Drum)

Violin I

Violin II

Viola

Violoncello

Bass

This overture was arranged by Edmund Haensch on themes from Offenbach's 1864 operetta La belle Hélène for a Berlin performance. The Berlin premiere was given around six months after the operetta's world premiere in December 1864. The present overture was most likely arranged for a late 19th century revival.

Duration: ca.8 minutes

© Copyright 2006 Clark McAlister
All rights reserved.

The large score and a complete set of parts are available for sale from Serenissima Music, Inc.

La Belle Hélène
Overture on Themes from the Operetta

JACQUES OFFENBACH
Arranged by Eduard Hænsch
Edited by Clark McAlister

* These instruments do not appear in Offenbach's original score and may therefore be considered optional.

Copyright © 2006 Clark McAlister.

15

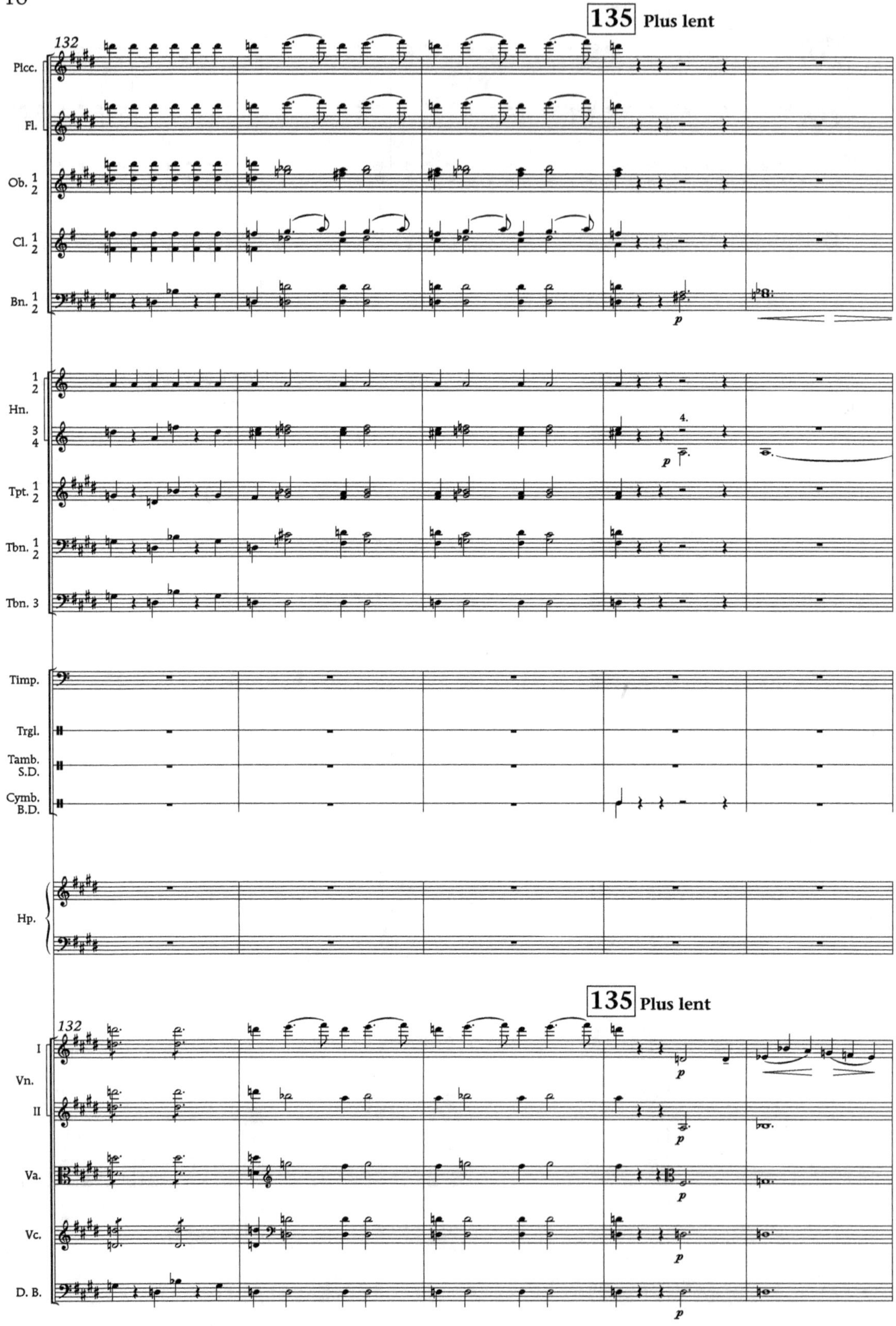
135 Plus lent
132
Picc.
Fl.
Ob. 1 2
Cl. 1 2
Bn. 1 2
p
Hn. 1 2 3 4
4.
p
Tpt. 1 2
Tbn. 1 2
Tbn. 3
Timp.
Trgl.
Tamb. S.D.
Cymb. B.D.
Hp.
135 Plus lent
132
Vn. I II
Va.
Vc.
D. B.
p

25

26

30

36

38

44